Sen.ti.ments:

a collection of hokku, tanka, onelinehaiku, and other short verses

by

SABAH (حابص)

FOREWORD

"I felt that I had to write. Even if I had never been published, I knew that I would go on writing, enjoying it and experiencing the challenge."

-Gwendolyn Brooks

"...I write to keep in contact with our ancestors and to spread truth to people."
-Sonia Sanchez

ACKNOWLDEGMENTS

There are so many individuals that have played parts in provoking me to finally get this work out of my blood. I'm very appreciative of you all. All honor to Yahweh, my God and Father and His Messiah, Yeshua the Christ...I'm thankful for even having this ability to fashion words into lasting images. Thank you Abba, for trusting me with this gift; as well as the others; for your honor and glory. Much respect, love, and deep gratitude to my mother, Pamela PreJean and my Pastor/Father, William L. Johnson II; you guys have done more for me than I could ever do for myself...hands down. To my other poets, writers, singers, actors, directors, and agents of the creative/artistic community; much thanks. I love you all. It's a privilege and a blessing to be creative, to be an artist. I hope you guys enjoy this...it's the fist of many. –Shalom!

PREFACE

It's been long overdue, but I'm finally churning out this book. My desire is to share with you my love for the little gem known as haiku (hokku). I'm not a master of haiku, I just love the simplicity and power of it.

I was introduced to haiku around 2005/06 right after the movie *Lovejones* came out. In the movie it was right after hearing Nia Long's character recite a poem by this poet with the name of Sanchez; that I began looking up information on the person and found the poet's name was Sonia Sanchez; a very prominent black American poet, playwright, activist etc. I was entranced by this woman's work, the passion, the sensuality and earthiness as well as the spirituality that pervaded each phrase she wrote. In Sanchez I saw myself. I saw a much more mature and sound me and I endeavored during that time to pattern my body of work after her…a true disciple. My introduction and love for haiku started with her and after six years here I am sharing my haiku (hokku) and other minimalistic poetic forms. My penname or 'haigo' is *Sabah* which is Arabic and Hebrew and respectively means 'dawn, morning' and 'aged man.' I wish you guys happy reading. Enjoy!

I.

HOKKU

grasping for life-
negro de la lluvia
in our footsteps

cante jondo-
our voices like our thighs
dancing black rain

bartered your love-
unfettered man catching my
pulse in warm hands

brocade laughter i
wear along my shoulders-
wind in tall grass

a long tapered kiss
entering the blood stream-
this imagery

ill wear devotion
well so when you arrive
you will enjoy it

wild winds against the
old mansion. a glass of port
drives the chill

with holy water –
bathing franciscan evenings my
lonely book to read.

what has become
of our days now awash with
neglect and tears

plum lamps
rich in color exploding
in our corneas

ill wear devotion
well so when you arrive
you will enjoy it

children's' sound raised on
corn and love- in her space
empty beds stand

louisiana
in her hips his lips; they both
cayenne this love-stew.

she sought this
non regal sound, I was
left seeking something.

he spoke in gregorian
chants...wearing aramaic
whispers; he settles.

met midnight
cement wilderness
your empty ways.

these private moments
when sky and clouds
hear my prayers.

you frame worlds
each time you breathe
in bronze laughter.

the first dawn
reading your rain. planting
our sound on old tin roofs.

in this breath
bound by money,
and by parents.

the face of his wife
grieving over 3rd child,-
he's at a loss for words.

making jokes
to hide
my torment.

incense smoke
reminds her of her need
for cigarettes.

a painted face in
MAC hiding ravages
of liver disease

me watching them
watch the homeless
man watch me.

he children still
see Auschwitz in
grandma's eyes.

the tenth in a
long line of men smiling
lies, staining my sex.

no longer sex traffic
slave, she flinches each time
a man looks at her.

pastor's son still
battling his need for boy's
with innocent eyes.

desperate for love
in a dark alleyway with
another faceless john.

day will see
us going to the market...
In shaa' Allah.

wore you, your
eyes rosaries, i pray
your breath amen

leaking faucet
a hymn to
my weary ears

in search of
Yahweh, mountain-God
of Horeb

passing the church
staccato 'hallelujahs'
walk the night air

overturned bowl
no trace of
the puppy

in a gown of
stars and cold
night welcomes.

man's yawn
carries during
contralto's cantata.

in bed alone
stroking to
diminish loneliness.

Henri LaBeaus' boy
near the bayou
making me woman.

in you
autumn whispers
lie dormant.

i imagine your
hand's trading
duetts with my blood.

mini-stanza

one step before
the other...
i, as is my
ritual; run
and hide hoping
the booze
causes you to
forget me...

there is nothing I
can offer
a heart beyond repair.

his eyes
translating prayers
in raindrops.

glass of sherry
brahms rhapsody
scribbling sonnets.

eyes widen-breath
catches...mouth
covers his need.

her rancor
offsets the sexy
negligee she wears.

yellow'd grass
breath of Yahweh
the green runs.

unspoken prayers
met the roof
of a closed mouth.

my teeth have
tutored my
tongue in restraint.

he was asked not
to depart her life his answer
his retreating shadow.

on my book-
case too many haiku
how-to books.

damaged girl
upstairs alone
tears mix with dust.

the old actress
drinking heavily speaking
of a glamorous past.

do we ease
into death with
working-class abandon.

speak my name outside
of sound-echo silence through
clenched teeth, now free me!

melody pours frm
ancient pores, druggin' tired minds-
move on winds of good.

cantor my breath
orchestra-i violin
mad scenes of life.

i torah - i exhale raw
need...can't tell what scribe
blew in my blood.

hokku sequence
(for Emmet L.Till)

1.

we taste the
blood ritual of
southern hands

2.

say no words...
time is collapsing
in the woods.

3.

your death
a blues i could
not drink away.

4.

mornin,' wind-priest speaks,
including life; calling
me into this day.

songku
(5755)

gingerly moving-
this one rhythm against the
other; our feet are
counter each other.

traverse this long stretch
of highway my impatience
rises as same car
cuts me off again!

started at the front
of yo book perusin' page
after page. i soak
up each verb each noun.

Yahweh, see me make
my way marchin' 'cross this dry,
and barren land of
life...see me come quick.

one loc extending
like the hand of a baby
stretched to be picked up;
except, beneath the
hair the scalp itches.

lonely white man, hunched
in the chocolate couch; no wor-
ries-just him waiting
for his friend to come.

'to do or not to
do?' my question. shld i run
these lines or engage
in writing songku?

some kind of feral
intensity you attack
the remaining break-
fast bagle; how rude!

on the stage of my
mind. lights dim and out i go;
mouth releasing the
tones of a mezzo.

from your bowels push
out the remnants of blue-black
wailin.' if night drinks
yo tears...i will too.

soil of life, my child…
bury your
feet in deep and sing

through an old window-
a breeze walks
through the airless room

after rain-
on the porch reading
the Septuagint

fighting
the urge to
call her

against
my brown skin...
-overcast skies

put away
    grandma's old dress
granddads approach

from the box
pulling out the old
marriage gown

child-like
clapping my hands—
...backyard

bowl of grapes
next to you
--the weekend

disloyal rain –
sea gulls drown your
confession

old siena—
choristers sing
in gregorian chant

casino lights—
neighborhood's quiet
stolen by cars

II.

TANKA

early mornin'
coffee and a
cigarette. gotta figure
out how come you
never come to me.

one
banana nut
muffin and dozens
of thoughts
about where you are.

when i
should be working
im typing tankas
about supposed
situations.

nestled
up to your
overly warm
form last night…
dreamed of peace.

capital one
high rise in the
center of town.
downtown pub calling
me for a drink.

everything about
you so whimsical
and healing...
two years later:
chile please!

met in the
back of a bistro
again the faint sound
of patchouli and
coffee.

what happened?
my questions met with
a cold silence. next
week we're laughing and
enjoying the fresh air.

two cyclist along
the access road while
I-10 teams with
hurried automobiles, a
stark contrast to them.

heading to work the
april sky crowned with
gray clouds in the east
i'm afraid to awaken
the neighbors lively dog.

at the PC quickly
learning to write tanka
from the best, but
ready to go get dinner
still my craft must grow.

taking a picture
beneath the old palm
we notice this
outdated sign saying
'Do Not Trespass'.

unable to eat
after finding your
closet empty.
tomorrow i see you
and you don't see me.

festival grins and
sparkling laughters on
the bleak air.
upstairs lying beneath
you wishing i could leave.

hunger pangs my
eyes catch the maroon
roof of the vistor's
beaureau. 6:50 and i'm
still typing out tanka.

green grass
cushion my back
and you move
in me right as rain.
later i hum gladness.

on this old
black stool eyes
seeing nothing.
later i'll move my
breath to a waltz.

casino in the distance
near the bridge
bringing your car.
we'll eat and dance and
i'll ride your midnight moans.

analog thinking
gives ripe swahili-bright sound
assessing this drab
noise that fills our earth.
silence: precious product.

shadow of empire state
loving you...the
taste of your moments
becoming mine
summer in the Apple.

wanted to fall in love-
but he's afraid he couldn't
match my
emotional/creative
intensity...so we just smile.

characterized life-
supposing i walk down wet
lanes, cars passing by
and for a moment, i pause-
...see reality clearly.

my work days are me
workin' and livin' the stretch
of synagogues-deep,
and pious...nearly sacred.
the pitch of being man.

yes, my man, time still
runs at break-neck speed; still out-
runs us, leaving us
tired and gripping the fleeting
nows with ironclad tenacity.

with pen, i memoir
the movement of our years. the
papyrus of skin
is forever and with deaf
eyes i see our story long.

its a tuesday work
day; to alleviate the
working ennui i will
multiply thoughts about you
in phrases that are colors deep.

over chianti--
lone toe traveling the length
of his calf-she smiles
wryly, he looks down-bursting
novas of emotion pour.

waiting...will the call
come? will my ears hear the lick
of a baritone
ebullience violently
arresting my inner ear?

high notes...singing these
'Hi' notes to your retreating
figure coming. guess
my brand of music is the
kind that's geared toward leaving.

this afro-black past
remembered is this black past
lived each now moment;
and for some reason
that black past, is more priceless-
the present is expensive.

III.

ONELINEKU

the dj's repetition of that song dulls my ears

afternoon traffic like long, stretched out boredom

around the dinner table no sound save chewing

and in the stale mississippi field her boys' lynched body

when approaching him im often swallowed in his night

with far away eyes seeing his brokenness and the stars

in the car she leans into my lap cradle my life

frantic calls to reserve rooms on my nerves people stay home

in my room ive yet to feel whats called peace of mind

my lonely room tonight ears pressed against silence

to leap beyond the fractured trail young girl and her lover

shaving my legs third time this week another gala

quietly stuffing eclairs in her mouth big ben chimes ten pm

to my left an unopened briefcase outside standstill afternoon

evaluating the men i keep claiming they never claim me

gripping the table masseuse kneading my back painfully

brief walk around the hotel mid afternoon breeze

spent an hour searching want-ads for a man and new stockings

palm leaves in the breeze wringing hands nervous against a magenta roof backdrop

asking me 'am i really intrusive?'

a mob of tourists boito sings on the phonograph

digesting food taking a walk raw leaves

unsatisfied with recycled dreams-cut down trees build new visions.

digesting food taking a walk

old orange juice crate your goodbye

locals around the hood are cute

dazed in sleep we'll attend a movie later

napping puppy chained outside

still pining for you the old house

ready to etch your touch in me

unrepentant morning i yawn

stretching baptized into day

my lack of imagination hasn't stopped me

ignoring sink full of dishes filtered sun

renegade enemas amid this symphony.

cedar mouths instigate where days bow.

playing in my locs, thinking serpentine thoughts.

his, a life of loose, un-tethered ends...tapestry.

wanted to endure the fresh taste of him .. his moment.

ashen lips utter early chants with quick feet I meet morning.

knew his lies, dogwood days stretching-his closet space empty.

bastard he left, humble he came. solidarity found in two oak trees.

look upon my silence. nurture my embers.

walks down old roads. he planted HIV her womb drowning.

(prostitutes ode)

a cabal of men sliding their hardened lusts between the legs of my satiation.

this south kat, alto sax pillage these eastern thoughts.

mid morning prayers to coffee grounds.

a taste of old regrets slightly decaffeinated.

lsley said: 'day will make a way for night...' watched you eyes bathing in your here.

he was tallis in flesh came with words draped in cambodian nights and reality.

became a prisoner to fascist love, slave to tyrannical passion.

with wide opened life, he lives. he breathes soundness.

your perennial laughter rising from our wine-dark soil.

holding my black brown yesterdays in tight lipped silences.

day is hard as the night you gather from the ancients words.

welcome home to my white seasons of knowing you.

drew life, real life from the lips of that tome...bless you Yahweh!

dingy curtains her eyes tracing the webs in the wall folds.

this patchwork moment. old buick mid afternoon sails.

memoirs read right to left. thoughts scrawled in elisions.

raped woman looking for bread crumbs of redemption light rain.

riding bass beats, your mannerisms kiss my open lungs.

stone gables and the freedom of dwelling in you...comfort.

wrapped in morning speaking monsoons walking turgid legs...hope.

in my mouth the taste of a low humming, our late talkings.

endorsed morning chants; slip from my tongue to the ground...fragrance.

dont push my love-cup aside, grab for the pewter indifference.

gripped me by my sight, exploited my reverence and words.

caught within the rain, playacting our deliverances.

He anoints my head with oil, my cup runs over.

and the coldness seeped thru young-old bones. young man awakens.

IV.

OTHER SYLLABLES

***sonku**

i watch you
slide down long
grins when
you produce
that knowledge

i listen
to the days
speakin'
slave-like speech...
but, its you.

hay(na)ku

sometimes
wooden words
termite my reason

tetrastich

carry
burning embers,
my loins sing
an arounsed concerto

quatrastich

on my back
blue memories
sail in and out
of a docked mind.

septastich

i babylon swollen
muslim glances...
and trail cool
orient fingertips
over persian-
loose hair.

**sonku – poetic form created by black American poet, Sonia Sanchez*

*sonku

i'll speak the
shadow of
your name when
you carve
'you' in my
tongue this day.

you invoke
wonder. i
paint mornin's;
each breath
distracts me.

walk silence
leaving me,
white washing
my love
until you
give me sound.

the worship
of where you
place your foot-
steps etched
in the soil
of my earth.

tetrastich

your chamber,
a cocoon
you emerge
with wings of fragrance.

pentastich

life's dirty laundry
of sullied shoes
are stamped into
those eyelids of the night
we lock those doors tight.

twowords

retched recriminations...

tristich

rancid thoughts
echo overt moans
of privilege.

tristich sequence

1.

peels of thunder trail
u mystic woman, phrase sorce'ry
raise blue ideas

2.

your ritual walk
peeling us into sasa/
fras laughter and tears.

3.

i will gas myself;
rose colored vapors of you...
we skip walnut dreams.

4.

boorish evening
silent cavorting to wild,
untamed men with words.

5.

bathed in day, my skin
breathes full, long inhalations
i dwell in cerulean peace.

septet #2

uptown man, yellow creole man...sun-kissed,
red flecks and bowed skies whistling against earth's
descant. i knew me. the silent walks I
took; exploring only those things the dark
concealed. considering eyes balanced be-
tween midnights, and the approaching morning.
in the distance this mezzo sings fluent.

abhanga #2
(her unspoken wish)

simple wish. just want a
man who consumes me. a
man who fashions one day
to adorn me.

sonnet

IV.

knew what incompletion felt like. once I
traveled extended years...journeyed through the
terrains of life giving of myself in
the hopes someone would reciprocate. knew
what giving all of me until I had
no more of me felt like. i lived it, most
of my life. eyes blinded by the brilliance
of fiber-glass stars accompanying
an imitation reality, and
for what? ive known the emptiness, ive drank
the bitter waters of nothing-else-to-
give. knew what incompletion felt like, tried
overlooking the loneliness. tried to
put up white-washed walls, like I had structure...
eventually I grew up, through the pain.

octaves I, II, III

I.

listen to it...incessantly begging...
asking, struggling, and pulling a refrain
that grates on the nerves. ears usually
deaf to the primal growl; my guilty hands
to blame for opening the door. what door?
portals to the never-fulfilled, bottomless
pit of lust. citizen of Nod, a real
wanderer praying for redemption's touch.

II.

waited near a setting sun. old woman
shuffling down Broad St. purse full of scorched
nostalgia; stockings torn. her air, one of
peace. ...was difficult waiting for me to
scrape off last evenings' fear. i hear her old
age-darkened voice peeling back pain, taking
the dirt of insecurities; telling
me to live, to boldly go, get and grow!

III.

I used to dream monochromatic. I
used to walk carrying a pocket-full
of un-jaded freedom. Freedom not grown
in the palm of hardship, cultivated
out of pain...i used to approach the sun,
my blatant blackness loud and un-contained.
then I was reckless and fresh...times before
I grew up; introduced to this REAL life.

sonnet

V.

monitoring my life...considering
my ways. taking the candle, light splashing
the darkened floors of this unexplored soul.
what will I see? will I be prepared to
meet the hidden things; face the ignored things?
the fall of twenty eleven, I...made
thirty; lights dancing before fresh, opened
eyes; I took an inward look at me; saw
me for the first time...saw the little me
cowering in corners of hurt, painted
with fears and distilled aggravations.
...glanced into the eyes of neglect, the air-
dampened with numbness; I pushed myself to
face myself...healing and wholeness entered...

septet

I.

aint nothing but a southern negro son,
a god-made aria, married to my art.
desperately searching out a place to plant
a sapling of sound and breath. looking for
a brief pause just to sing...you know? that pause
to collect my tunes and bury them, spread
my own song across a thirsty earth-scape.

rhyme-royal

I.

down Lexington and 45st street he
walked the walk of men condemned, that dead-walk.
passed me by, heard this swallowed 'hello.' seen,
that dangerous look, empty eyes that stalk.
it was May; the air full of peoples' talk
and he made it to her place. No greetings
only cold glances...sound of birds singing.

II.

i was a boy-man making men hobbies.
married to insecurities. i would
misplace my right to think; my body leased
loneliness I wore, reaching what I could;
I indwelled this structure blackened wood...
a house intended for empty mem'ries
and me trying to find those living keys.

V.

EXTRAS etc.

rigid afternoon—
...easy sex in the
photo shop

dinner
with a turkish pasha...
--slick streets

dank harbor:
...we're still going
dancing

moment's blight—
painting the house slowly

you,
empty shell.
a woman unseen

feeding a puppy passing car

outside in a blue robe overcast skies

dreamed of touching you cicada song

wash away my insecurities in the sea of your kisses

the dark is my delight dulcimer plays

what follows is indifference pale morning

in his eyes bitter moments in honey

door ajar sounds of Basie while mopping

loud tv competes with his snoring

evening chill in need of your pulse

ready lies in my vermilion womb

filtered words hitting linoleum ears

afterglow listening to his chartreuse whispers

hollow my womb, dusky diamonds and jazz

remove the straps of clothing this eve

late night walking the curve of sleepiness

some nights i gravitate toward the moon

her womb a stone labriynth cold chills

the sky's blue feet across your thigh

face to face bathtub of dry gin

a mob of tourists boito sings on the phonograph

digesting food taking a walk

old orange juice crate your goodbye

locals around the hood are cute

dazed in sleep we'll attend a movie later

napping puppy chained outside

still pining for you the old house

ready to etch your touch in me

unrepentant morning i yawn

stretching baptized into day

my lack of imagination hasn't stopped me

ignoring sink full of dishes filtered sun

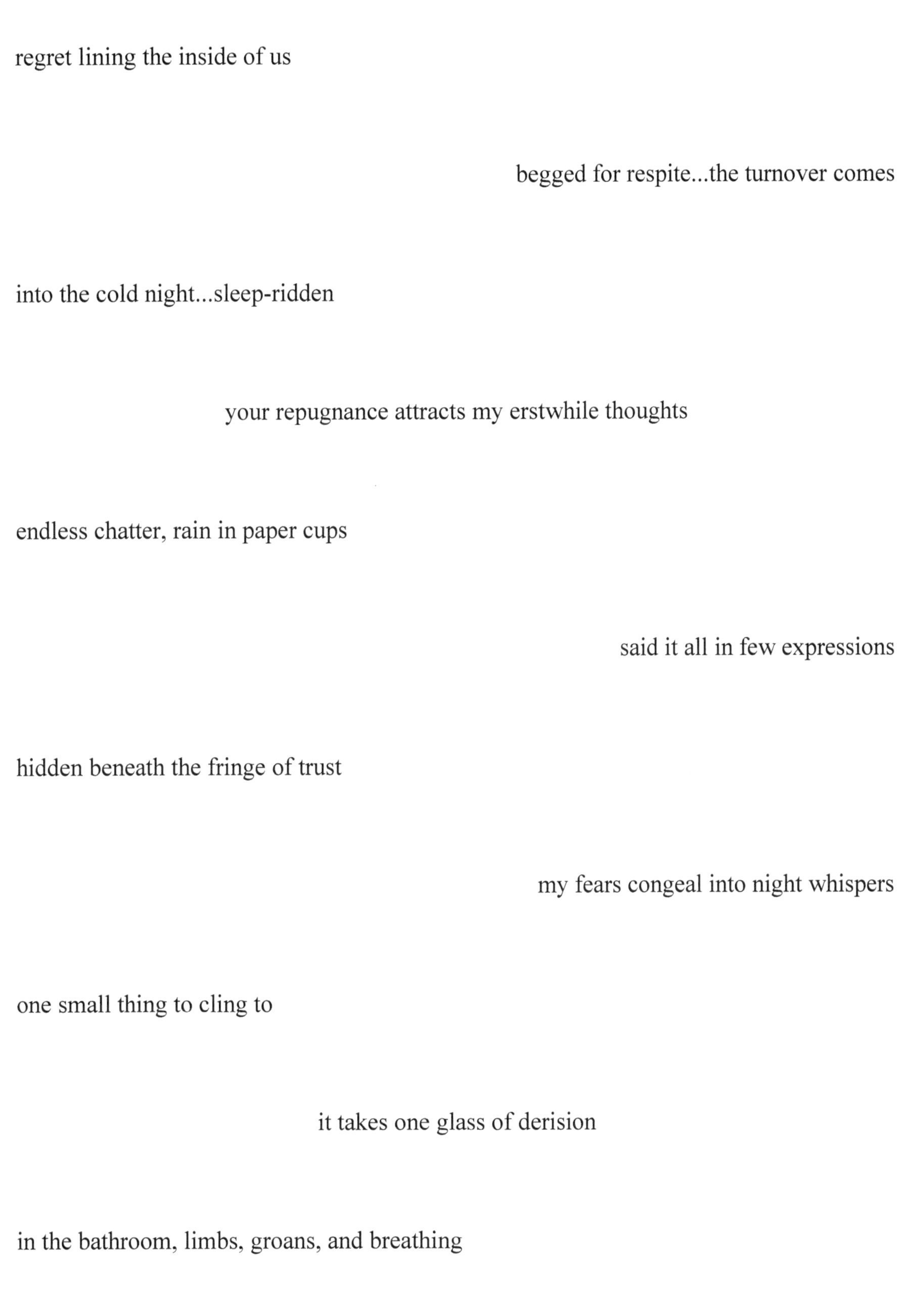

SIX/SEVEN word stories

regret lining the inside of us

begged for respite...the turnover comes

into the cold night...sleep-ridden

your repugnance attracts my erstwhile thoughts

endless chatter, rain in paper cups

said it all in few expressions

hidden beneath the fringe of trust

my fears congeal into night whispers

one small thing to cling to

it takes one glass of derision

in the bathroom, limbs, groans, and breathing

we spoke of sex in covered tones

she wore indifference, like last seasons' fur

there's nothing casual when you beat me

we, repressed boys trying to be men

gravitating toward the sophistication of noble simplicity

picant brother. salsa in my hips....savory

[*greatest 'love' story*]

she fell.
his bed, his unrevealed side.

sing in off-key voice to the sun.

love given, though i whore eagerly...Yahweh

my evenings bowed...we pas de deux.

[sevenwordstory]
(to Abba Yahweh)

...i'll feel the brush of His, His-ness

deep in my soul; a'runnin' after You

my soul; womb for your commands

...when Your reason kissed my finite mind

aged socialite, me gigalo; entrepreneurial endeavors

lost soul begging me for defining

go the way your blood beats

watched emotions scatter across your brow

yet ignored by the autumn whispers

i was never fond of your daddy

[sixwordstory]
(*Abba Yahweh*)

came to You for complete change

walk'd away. sin displeases. new life

planted in Your breathing-i'll flourish

Yahweh hooked me, now i'm hooked

****finis****

…thank you for enjoying my scribings.

-SABAH (حابص)

Contact Information:

twitter: @SABAH_81
facebook: http://www.facebook.com/TheWayfarer81
email: SABAH1981@live.com

www.ingramcontent.com/pod-product-compliance
Ingram Content Group UK Ltd.
Pitfield, Milton Keynes, MK11 3LW, UK
UKHW051134260726
13967UKWH00010B/3053